I0407439

Fixing America in Twenty Years:

Can It Be Done?

By

Lonnie Hicks

ISBN- **ISBN-13:978-1500838461**

ISBN-10: 1500838462

Copyright 2014

F ixing America What Needs To Be Done

What Does America Need To Do To Survive?

The first area to look into is those pillars of American success I identified above: Cheap Labor, Cheap Energy, Cheap Food and a country filled with natural resources.

Who is killing these pillars and why?

The greatest negative influence on these three pillars of American property in the last five years has been Wall Street and the major banks.

The pillars are:

1-**Cheap Food**: The last nail in the cheap food pillar in the United States was in 2008 when Goldman and other investment bankers entered the wheat market and bought long thereby inflating wheat prices from an historic 3 dollar level up to 15 dollars. This resulted in food riots around the world, since the United States supplies the bulk of the world's wheat. They are still there making billions off these artificial food shortages bringing food insecurity to millions, not only around the world but in the United States as well.

2-**Cheap Energy:** The same scenario is true for energy, espec ially oil. Wall Street and the bankers drove the price of oil from 25 dollars a barrel to 125 dollars a barrel and the cost at the pump from 1.25 a gallon to nearly3-4 dollars currently. Our cheap energy price went up and has stayed up. Now these same two robber barons are poised to make money on the cap and trade market. Who is going to profit from cap and trade as a solution to the energy and pollution problems--the large banks and Wall Street.

3- **Cheap Labor:** Labor used to be cheap because the cost of living in the United States was low. A single wage-earner could support the family.1968 was the last year in which real wages increased. Since then it has gone down meaning now the wife is working and the kids can't find a job at all, and on top of that, the kid is competing for a job with grandmother who is sometimes, supporting the kids and the grandchildren.

The college educated child can find no job. Fifty percent of all college graduates come home after graduation, not finding a job. This kind of under-employment and unemployment is the bank and Wall Street way of keeping labor costs low. People will work for pennies to support their families.

Given this recent history we need to look at what are the other influences and the history of these pillars and then on to specifics on what needs to be done to solve these problems.

To the list I will now add, a decent birth rate or immigrant flow, small town and technical green enclave investment, income distribution reform, land distribution reforms, banking and financial reforms and a re-thinking of the purposes of an economy.

Cheap labor built this country, from the Chinese coming to lay the track for the railroads, to the Africans working the cotton in the South, to the immigrants from Europe who cleared the land in the west, who worked the factories, fought the wars and made America what it is today.

Needless to say the labor scene is not the same today. Cheap labor has been outsourced to other countries.

The American middle class has not only been abandoned but 40% of American savings were taken from them and their homes, their major asset, are now selling for half the purchase price to those very same interests which took the savings and the land.

We are heading for a two class system, therefore, the rich and the poor. Certainly that is the pattern becoming evident in many of our cities.

In addition, there is the lack of labor, cheap or otherwise, which is the demographic issue. Americans are not having children, nor are the Europeans and the demographics are becoming clear: by 2060, some demographic studies show, the reproducing populations of Russia, Britain, France and Italy will, in essence, cease to exist and the traditional populations will be replaced by immigrants from other countries. The same trends are evident in the United States as well. Latin American birth rates outstrip those of Americans and demography becomes destiny, in a flice.

So, as we age in this country, we see a younger population replacing an older one, of a very different stripe. Our children will learn more Spanish in the short-run but English will have resurgence in the next generation. What is to be done in this context is now our challenge.

The first issue in the short run is the economy. The country will, and already has, in certain communities become a two-economy society. Why should I, nor can I, compete for basic living necessities with individuals earning 2-3 times more than I do?

A two-economy solution, whether created or defacto-realized seems inevitable. The rich will likely not be allowed to shop in the second economy where the price of necessities can be artificially raised in a so-called "free market." This solution creates a low-cost economy of necessities for those who provide the labor. This makes sense and many do this to survive anyway today. Thrift shops, discount stores, Walmarts all attest to the fact that the middle class cannot afford middle class and upper middle class prices. Devastatingly, 40 million Americans are now on food stamps and millions more on Medicaid. This is horrible.

The second pillar of revamping the labor force (the one above creates an economy which works for them) is to have that labor force become more self-sufficient and not be susceptible to being wiped out by Wall Street machinations and global trends in faraway countries. This means the re-claiming of productive land and small towns where they can be supportive of a laboring population. Bartering, co-ops, low living costs, plus a land reform policy can make the country-side more productive and sustainable especially in the context of greening these small towns to produce energy for re-sale to the grid.

Believe it or not Detroit is trying this approach. Tear the decorated buildings down, down-size the city, allow for population loss, put in self-sufficient gardening and farming plots, bring in technological enclaves. This is an admission that the city model does not work, at least in Detroit.

Now you have idle workers in small towns all over the country. We can make those small towns productive with massive investments. How you say is that possible? More tomorrow.

February 18, 2010 - Survival Chapter Three

As, I have stated elsewhere our children, will not be able to afford the suburban home of the past.

In the cities they will be forced and are, already, living three to five a house or apartment. High unemployment will remain with us and a revamping of the economy from a service emphasis to a new high-tech, green emphasis will take time. What to do. Here are a few modest proposals about what to do with the labor force, idle out there and hurting.

1-Create a **massive internal peace corp.** Put people to work re-vamping small towns for their change-over to a more self-sustaining model. This includes local organic food stuffs, grown and consumed. Free up land for this purpose. People will grow gardens. Put money into green training and irrigation projects. Bring people languishing unproductively in the cities back into these very same small towns. Bring back and support local and regional banks and co-ops of various kinds, crops, loans, machinery, techno co-ops can work if local.

Remember what happens when we allow Wall Street to become our bankers?. Take those same highly educated city grads, currently living five to an apartment, and give them money to go back home to their own small towns, or others to help set up the infrastructure needed to fuel this internal peace corps re-generation of America. Move people out of the cities with incentives to go back to the small town or the medium sized town. We have technology now where we don't need to congregate in cities to be productive, that was an industrial model where you needed the labor force close and available near ports and transportation hubs. We don't need this so much in this postindustrial era. Has this model been tried? Sure. Dependent wage-earners in the city are an economic failure. We should admit it and go local and regional.

The poor won't be poor if they are given the means to access the basics of life. The middle class can revert to the community help model that is still in place in many small towns, and has been for centuries. After all, most of the world was a small town model until populations were forced into the cities to serve the needs of robber barons. Now the second aspect of reform is to take the **technological enclaves** I have described and integrate them into what I have described above. I have noted that much of the information revolution is actually driven by a few high skilled enclaves around the world and by relatively few people. They are Silicon valley-like enclaves in California, China, Singapore, France, Germany, Hong-Kong etc. These enclaves are small towns where participants know one another and exchange ideas. This is the second model of small town regeneration. These **type two** small towns are to be in contact with **type one small towns** and can become training cadres for small town re-generation. How? Give them tax breaks to do so and guess what they will have at their disposal; cheap labor from the sources we identified above. That is what we need to do in the short run, town by town.

So we have a new source of cheap labor, idle now but which can become productive again. Empty the cities, get people out of what are inefficient enclaves and get them to places where the population can begin to benefit itself not a few hundred thousand rich souls who control city life.
Ah, not possible you say? The choice here is stark: Either we organize this new re-generation by planful means or it will occur in an unplanned way, which is to say people abandoning the cities and invading the country side looking for the means to survive. Be mindful here that any disaster of any meaningful proportions will initiate this process anyway and we will not have planned for it
A last stark fact: The average grocer has three days' worth of food on the shelves. People will invade the country side looking for food and this will be the plan I just discussed being initiated the hard way. And that is ugly.

The collapse of centralized authority, unplanned, happened with the collapse of the Roman Empire, initiating the Dark Ages, and happened, in fact, in the bible as I have argued above, and happened with the collapse of Egyptian rule in Canaan. It happened with Katrina. Any breakdown from natural or man-made sources will create the pattern I describe above.

February 22, 2010 "What Does America Need To Survive?" Chapter 4

Have there been other examples of civilizations abandoning the city as unworkable; or central authority collapsing, of abandoning empire as unworkable? The Mayans abandoned pyramid building, the Greeks, the Babylonians, the French, the British, the Romans, countless examples. Most large scale centralized authority systems fall down. They are not generally pulled down. The most recent example is that of the Russians who abandoned their empire as unworkable.

It is part of a normal pattern.

Now to get to the detail: Include the army in the small town regeneration project, along with the young and the college-educated. Many of them have ties to these small towns and it would be a home coming. Have the technological enclaves close by with small towns providing labor in exchange for training. Isn't that what the Army does anyway? Focus efforts in regeneration on greening and self-sufficiency. These will be key. This would mean small truck farms, wind, solar and the techno-enclave would be in proximity; and, ultimately, able to produce energy for the gird.

Of course, there will be a fight over the land. Currently developers, banks, railroads, utilities and the US government own most of the land in the country. There would have to be a new land use policy. Survival is at stake. But the fight could be won because small states dominate in the US Senate and a deal could be struck because their states would benefit from such a plan.

Think of it. Most of the wasted resources in this country are utilized keeping the cities afloat. They are not economic, crime ridden, have no real products they produce, have teeming unemployment looming and bound to get worse and net resource wasters. They demand massive investments in transportation, food, energy and give little back in terms of long-term sustainability. Young people: the idle, the technologically advanced are better utilized on the country-side landscape.

Just a thought.

Cheap labor is possible to put back into the American equation. As I am fond of saying, this will happen well and planned or ill-planned and ugly.

February 26, 2010 "Survive"
The next item in tandem is **cheap energy**. Above we have mentioned wind and solar. We add to the list battery power, and plasma power. There are ideas around the idea of clean coal and cheap oil, but we are better off looking at fuel substitutes that include vegetable oils and other grain based fuels. At the very least stockpiles ought to be created for the emergencies which will surely come in the future. But will all this be enough, timely and efficient in the face of climate change, aging populations, declining incomes, looming depression, and political paralysis?
Such timing is critical, the answer is unknown. However, we have no choice in the energy field; we must act as if we will succeed. The overall goal is clear; create a society which city and country-side produce net energy give-backs to the grid.
Friends of mine stated part of the problem succinctly, "Why re-build an outmoded infrastructure; build the new one directly."
On the energy level the task is a delicate one: We have to build the boat we are sailing to Europe on while sailing to Europe. The reason that this is even to be looked at is that you can do this if you build the boat as a series of rafts

strung together. Those rafts are small towns. Seen this way, it is possible to accomplish the task. Of course there is not enough money in the world to re-build the old infrastructure, but a green infra-structure is possible under scenarios I outline below. That structure is cheaper in the long run, more competitive, locally controlled and has cheaper labor costs, as I have outlined above.

The next issue is **cheap food.** America has long been the bread basket of the world but that small-farmer model of production has long been replaced by big agriculture which now means genetic farming where corn itself has reduced strains available and most of them owned, repeat, owned by the Monsanto's of the world. It is illegal to grow the corn without their permission. And to boot Monsanto has created grain strains which can only be planted once and is bad for people as well. Rat experiments show genetically altered food cause serious problems in humans. This is being ignored.

This, of course, changes the cheap food equation. If grain seed and indeed water, and the very air can become private property then the house of cards will collapse. Clearly this system is not sustainable and is not viable as a public good. Re-generation will have to be accompanied by a re-thinking of who owns food grains. Who owns water, land, air? It is instructive to even have to discuss these issues this way. What hath progress wrought?

How can food be re-democratized? It will have to be. Hungry people will find a way to feed their families and Monsanto and their patents will have to stand aside and let people grow whatever they want.

Now a potential catalyst in all of this are returning veterans from our two wars. (War is a form of employment which is why it so easily becomes popular.)

These folks, having made sacrifices for the country will come home, assuming the wars end, will need jobs and there are none. They will need medical care, in a medical system which is broken. They will need re-training, in a country which is cutting college budgets. Something similar happened after World War One and those vets marched on Washington. It can happen again. These might as well when they and their families find they cannot make a living once back home. They are good candidates for re-generation projects where living costs will be lower and green re-training possible.

But the potential volatility of that issue remains. The two-economy solution will become more apparent with these veterans back home. After all, we have an example of this with the military itself where the internal military economy runs on its own terms not those of the general American economy.

So what then is the next issue to be solved? We need to look at small town economic models and their regional counterparts. Tomorrow.

February 27, 2010 "Survive"
The economic picture is glum, but things will sort themselves out well or badly. Let's concentrate on well. The first item many of you have mentioned is the issue of where will the money come from to institute many of the ideas I have outlined above. Bob mentioned the national debt, two wars, and a trillion dollar deficit. All true . The national debt is 12.4 trillion dollars and soon the interest payments against that debt will be the second largest item in the national budget.

What will happen? What can happen? Can we or our children pay this debt? No, not right now.

What will likely happen is either default or re-structuring. We owe the money to the Chinese and the Japanese and the banks mostly and we will likely simply restructure with all and create new lower payments. The Japanese and the Chinese will likely will agree, to the extent they can see their exports increase to us in our re-generation efforts here.

They could get some debt funds paid back in that way, along with currency re-valuation in the Chinese example. And guess who will be in China, utilizing that cheap labor-US companies who can produce for the US market utilizing this foreign labor and also help create that green market back home as well. This has synergy. Sloppy synergy but yes synergy. Inevitable? No. But a logical path.

The two wars have cost about 1.2 trillion and have to be wound down slowly so as to not exacerbate all those towns dependent upon military contracts in the United States and all those countries dependent upon US military bases abroad. (There are 745 such bases scattered around the world.) We are a war-dependent economy seeking to become a peace economy that will take time, say 20 years.

So the first step in economic re-generation will be the global changes described above from the perspective of the United States. We can't pay the debt and, in some cases, (bank debt) should not be paid. Besides we need the money for the internal changes above or we pay in internal disruptions from economic chaos if we don't act. Think 20 rolling Katrina's due to water shortages in one case, food shortages in another case, rising inflation which make the dollar worth a lot less, transportation breakdowns, terrorist attacks etc.

We are a fragile over-technologized society, and so interdependent that five airplanes can bring our economy to its knees. This is not good.
Now the small town answer here is, therefore, a good idea not only for economic reasons but for strict military reasons as well. Ninety-five percent of the people living on one percent of the land is a bad idea militarily. Disbursement is a better idea.

Now the mix we are talking about here is one of small-town, regional and yes some cities where cities make sense. But the basis of the American future has to be local, upgraded with technology, not massed populations in vulnerable cities. Re-generation is re-building America from the bottom up and abandoning top-down systems. So how much time will this all take and what are the barriers?

March 1, 2010 "Survival"

A wise sage once said "What to do is easy, but the first step of what to do is the problem." The same is true here. The answer to the question of how long we have to accomplish certain critical first steps is a function of how long will the first steps take. And what are those first steps? Here we go:

The country has to be put on a disaster footing, whether that disaster is any of the calamities I have described above or someone not yet conceived. Here is what I think we have to do, over what time line, with what human power sources and at what cost:

1-Just as we have voting booths and places in every community in the United States we must do the same for the regeneration effort. We will need in an emergency, power, medical, housing food, water, and energy and ways to move people efficiently. We partially have this in place with F.E.M.A but I would not bet my life on their help, would you?

The first scenario is the three to--five day survival period. In a disaster we want people to be self-sufficient and be able to survive for at least three-to five days after an event or in general:

--That is every home must have five days of food, non-perishable (remember, we assume no power will be available)

--Each home must have or access to five days of clean water
--Each home must have access to an emergency medical kit
--Each home must have a shortwave radio kit or access to same
--Each home must have a fuel generation kit, assuming gasoline supplies will quickly become depleted
--Each home must have access to the ability to produce heat or fire
--Each home must have a tent for temporary shelter if necessary.
--Each home must have seed grains for a vegetable garden (yes, let's think ahead)
--Each home must have a 12 volt battery, an auto battery will do and, add two bicycles, and a crowbar and rope.
--Each block must have a disaster warden, someone who would get training in the above items and their use; a paid position.

Right now some homes have these items, most don't. Some communities have their processes in place, some don't. Shopping list item one for the state and federal government: have our re-generation work force, (remember these folks?) create "Survival Support Kits" on every block in America. Kit production will provide jobs; make survivability a real option for Americans not only for natural disasters but other kinds of slow degeneration from economic collapse as well.

These kits will be on every block, or within walking distance and supplement those home supplies I have described above. Why all this effort? The worst thing you can have is millions of people in the cities on the move after five days looking for food or trying to escape the chaos of the cities.

There are massive issues with this kind of movement. You want folks to hunker down in place and survive for at least five days to ten days until state or federal efforts can be mounted.

Hunkering down also makes security for these communities easier, rather than dealing with a scattered population on the move.
The details of how you get fuel without gasoline I will spare you but survivalists know them well.
 How much will this effort cost? Unknown, but my guess is each kit and its mobile container will cost in materials about 750 dollars. Labor costs would be about 500 per kit, transportation, training and placement and after support: about 2,500 dollars per kit for the first year. Let's add contingency costs and the kit total is 5,000 per unit. How many units? Let's say a million units installed in each of five years: 25 billion total.

Of course there are other costs as well. All we have here is survival days one through five. But what about after the five to ten day period I have postulated. But note this is not just a five-day survival plan it is the first step toward local self-sufficiency. More on that tomorrow.

March 2, 2010 "Survival"

All of the above effort gets us five to ten days of sufficing, mostly in the city. Beyond the ten-day mark there is a lot more to do. Moreover, what I have described above is mostly related to the cities. The country-side effort is presumed to be in place from the other efforts described above and will have similar outlines as the city effort except that the Army, state and federal forces will lead that effort.

After ten days cities will be out of food and masses of individuals will head toward the country-side to escape what will be an increasingly chaotic and dangerous city environment; people use guns to get what they need, looting, dogs running in packs, sanitation issues erupt right away. Terrible..

These patterns of behavior are not uncommon; we see them in every prolonged disaster or emergency.

Most of these ideas work in fire, earthquake, terrorist action, drought, power failure, water issues etc. They are not great for nuclear war. There all bets are off.

Now in the country-side you have to have in place before the above disasters or slowly degenerating circumstances (the latter is more likely) reception centers to receive the city dwellers. Housing, kits, medical attention, sustainability planning all will have to be done before hand. The kits I speak of have to be along major exit routes and highways out of the urban areas and final destination points have to be marked out before hand to handle millions of people.

Food stuffs, water purification, temporary governmental functioning, security issues, communication, transportation and mobility-- all issues that this country has not acted upon and may have to.

A slow moving degeneration of our financial systems is the easiest to deal with. But think back to October 1929. The collapse of the stock market put millions on the road looking for food and work. Then most people had country cousins who grew food. Today this is not the case today. This can happen again and we have done nothing to anticipate or prepare.

What will a truly national or even regional effort look like? We build that infrastructure block by block, city by city, region by region focusing our effort based on what areas, cities or regions have the best sustainability components and spend money in those areas which do not.

The haves are put to work creating sustainability for the have-nots.

But details and costs loom here. How can this be done in the next twenty years-an arbitrary time period, but one I think is the last window we have to have gotten much of this in place.

We create hubs, local and regional until a national network is in place. The jobs it will create will help. The products, all aligned with sustainability and green goals give the country a future in the global economy, and we come out if it stronger militarily and mentally.

But as always the question is what comes first, who does it, how much will it cost and how effective will this effort be?

March 3, 2010 "Survival"

The mounting of a national effort encompassing a local, regional and country-wide effort will take twenty years. It will involve a simultaneous re-vamping of the American economy and political structure such that local self-sufficiency to the maximum degree possible is built into the new system. Our issues with infra-structure, energy, power, food etc. are all based upon the assumption that the present system will be in place when clearly the present system needs to be totally re-conceptualized.

The maxim is that with every complex system at some point there simply isn't enough brain power at the top to manage systems when they reach a certain size, no matter how much technology we throw at it.

The dream that we could automate our way to a well-run system is a dream. It happens over and over again with empires, cities and even small regions. People run systems best who are close to the production of its basic outlines.

What if I were President? What would I do? Well the American people, and others in other countries, do not really believe that life can change from what it currently is. We are paralyzed into complacency, feel powerless to change anything and not sure if we really want to see much change. As one of my students said, "Will I still be able to still play piano?"

Now the first thing I would do is to shake up the situation with new Federal law that would place in each American home the basic needs I have outlined above for the first line of defense in the event of an emergency in American cities. Each home or block would receive one of the kits I describe at a cost of five hundred per kit.

This is the "wake-up call" approach. Things have to be shaken up. Kick the mule to get his attention. This is a signal that we as Americans are vulnerable to various emergencies and must make preparations. I would bill it as the first steps toward local control and de-centralization, away from centralized banks and financial systems to more local ones, to more local political and social control, to a more self-sufficient country; re-building America from the bottom up and creating new self-sufficiency green and smart jobs.
This is true re-organization and cheaper by far than the current centralized system which mostly benefit, life-time politicians, lobbyists and the rich.
That is America's future if America is going to survive and compete in the global economy of the future. If this is not done the current situation where the top five percent of the population has control over more wealth that the bottom ninety-five percent will create social unrest of enormous proportions and a re-alignment will occur through the messy method and social unrest, rather than through the ways I am proposing here. Let's hope we all come to our

senses.

Update June 15, 2010

An interesting question here is how do the re-generation principles above match up with an actual emergency, such as the BP oil spill? The above was written before the spill but it provides an example of what is happening and how, if a re-generation plan had been in place, things would be different.

First we have a spill, the largest in American history which will contaminate over 1/3 of the Gulf of Mexico, is an environmental disaster, will affect the livelihood of thousands along the coast and inland as well, among some the poorest states in the Union. Unemployment, damaged tourism, and decay will be with the regions for years.

And to boot we are treated to a scene where politicians parade across our TV screens promising relief but delivering none, in it mainly to get their faces on TV and hoping thereby to get re-elected, no FEMA springs into action, and payments have to come from BP and meantime how are people going to feed themselves, and make boat and house payments? A mess.

Now under re-generation, first of all, BP would be required to click a computer screen and transfer a few billion dollars directly to local banks who where the individuals involved could draw upon. This would take a few minutes. Right now they are sending checks after a claims process.

But we have no local banks. Besides the politicians want credit for relief because that means votes for them. Too quick relief and they become irrelevant.

Local banking structures who have the house note and the boat note could and would be in place under regeneration. There is no substitute for a local person who knows each individual in the community and their needs. If BP didn't transfer the money then the Federal Reserve or the Federal government should or under re-generation would be required to.. It is a down payment on ultimate claims but people in an emergency need money now, not later. Have I mentioned local co-ops? They are even better than local banks but many don't have the electronic transfer technology to handle some transactions and don't hold the mortgages and boat notes. Credit unions are also good choices, but same problem. We have to build these under re-generation.

Second, given what is a slow moving disaster a livelihood for millions has now been destroyed. Where will they find work? Many, as was the case with Katrina will abandon the old jobs and livelihood and we will see decay, boarded up business and migration. Under re-generation a self-sufficient plan would be in place to have those unemployed be employed locally in techno and small town enclaves and available for disaster relief. There would have been a plan B. There is no plan B now in place in the Gulf and there was no plan B; and there is no plan B even being planned for the Hurricane season upcoming.

Hurricane season: Boy is there a need for plan B. When the winds arrive what hopes for a return to normalcy might be dashed and millions will be in need or at least on the move.

Are we preparing? Nope. The states say we have no money. The Fed says BP is going to pay; BP is going to say hey, the people responsible for rig safety are registered in the Marshall Islands and can't be touched. A court battle will take years and people will be long discouraged or gone and nobody will in the end will take responsibility.

The moral of this tale is clear: Communities have to plan for self-sufficiency against man-made and natural disasters. Plan for food, energy, and the labor force to rebuild or sustain what is in place. The large entries, the government, BP etc. can't and don't have an interest in helping. It is not profitable for the oil company to give away too much money, and is useful to the politicians only in as much as they can get votes out of it for the next election. After that they move on to the next photo op.

We have to think that the self-sufficient frontier societies of 150 years ago have to be wedded to the techno innovations of today to keep this country going and for it to thrive. Be sure to write your congress person.

June 20, 2010

Now that BP has come up with 20 billion the first interesting point is that it could not deliver the funds directly or quickly to the people who need it. No, they gave the money to the US government. Be prepared for a long wait while the state and local politicians hop a plane to Washington to see if they can get their hands on that money and control of its distribution so as to dole it out to friends, supporters who can help them get re-elected while the people in the gulf deplete their life savings, go into debt, search for other work, prepare for cleanup which might last years, contemplate that 1/3 of the gulf being poisoned, while the marshlands affected by the spill die and make the land areas more vulnerable to hurricanes just months away.

Things ain't going so swell.

So what to do?

First get the money out of the US hands to local banks and /or co-ops formed by the communities themselves, composed of the members of that community. (A pipe dream I know) But some people have formed communities and they ought to be encouraged.

Secondly, a regional disaster recovery plan ought to be instituted following the steps I have outlined above. (Has anyone heard from FEMA lately?)

We ought to be hiring the unemployed and the skilled to go down to institute the plan on a regional basis. First we need to implement the short term emergency plan I outlined about while simultaneously instituting the long term plans I identified. Note here the ability of residents in the area to earn a livelihood from the Gulf may be affected for many years. A new plan for the small towns in the area has to be created So what is to be the new self-sustaining model for the area? Obviously the last plan of depending upon the sea and tourism didn't work so well.

I like the idea of desalination of the sea, solar power and water power from the Gulf. Make the hurricanes pay for themselves by harnessing the wind to produce electricity. Just a thought. Here would be cheap energy, cheap labor and we could introduce elements of cheap food.

Will this happen? Only God knows, but I would not take odds on it.

July 13, 2010

We had a score card on what is needed to turn America around, avoid disaster, and save our widows and orphans. So how are things going?

1- The Gulf: Not so good. We have delay after delay and we have not only one disaster but many. The Hurricane season is now, to peak in September. Are we prepared? No.

Citizens still don't have the money they need to survive not to mention repairs to their lives and cities and even if that hurdle was surpassed there is the matter of fishing and livelihoods all gone for the time being. BP is borrowing money and trying to sell assets because of the spill and that means no new or on-going help from them.

The marshlands are gone. This is a slow moving disaster, but, a sure one.

Are housing, disease, schools, state finances, re-building efforts kicking in or likely. Nope.

Score card F

2- The new Financial Reform bill coming through the Senate is a bust. It does not change much and the current wall-street depression will happen again. Why because the European Union has trillions is debt due in 2012 and no way to pay it So do we. That means trouble for you and me because American banks and other central banks will pay themselves first, and bring us the bill. We, as taxpayers, are last in the que. Therefore, we are looking at no loans, likely inflation, and more austerity programs and lay- offs and unemployment. "You folks," the mantra will go, "have to tighten your belts."

Who can afford a belt?

Score Card Financial: F

If you don't want to be cheered up any further, skip the next section because things get worse.

3-Unemployment: Millions are now on tender hooks waiting for Senators demanding payoffs for their states for supporting the unemployment extension, meantime the unemployed suffer, many times after having spent a *life-time paying unemployment insurance*. Someone please explain what happened to all the excess funds in the unemployment funds, both state and national? Spent. That's what.

Now the cruel aspect this unemployment season is that wall street, and the banks take our money (remember we deposited money in their banks every day and they took that money and gambled it, lost part of it, took the profits after hedging our funds, made millions, and greed upon greed, took 40% of the values of our middle class homes and 40% of our 401k and now benefit from this employment cycle because cheap labor is back--five applicants for each job, depressed wages, and those with jobs work long hours knowing that there are five people who will take that no- raise, reduced benefit, position they currently have.

Let's be clear: Who does unemployment benefit and who has the money to buy up our de-valued assets at pennies on the dollar--the same folks who took those assets, and get this, used our own money against us, and if there are any losses in all of this, they can simply use government funds to get paid for those losses--if you are a bank--getting paid with money that was is our money again-essentially we are covering banking losses incurred using our money in the first place. The FDIC will collapse. No one can cover the trillions in losses here.

I told you this would be depressing.

Despite all of this we ask what can be done? Well there are some critical things, but now you should have a headache, I do, and need some sleep.

Tomorrow: Hint: A solution is not to put another gang in charge to take their turn at feeding at our trough-meaning Republicans.

July 15, 2010

Hello all. What is to be done? Well can't do it all today but here are some quick effective items. These are things which may seem unconnected but are not:

1- First the power of the banks and Wall Street derive directly from us citizens and the fact that each day we give them our money to play with and gamble with. The first step is don't do that.

a. Move your money from the big four banks to a local bank, co-op or credit union. That keeps it local and denies the beast the money-food it uses against you.

b. Every day you give money to Wall Street through your 401k. Don't do that. Keep yourself liquid; keep the cash. There is not going to be any interest on your money for years anyway. Keep it at home. It denies the beast the money it uses against you.

c. Create your own local bank (that is what a coop is.) Your money stays home and is safe. No Wells Fargo, No Bank America, No Citbank, No Chase. (Note all of our local banks are dying. Revive them and make them work for you. If you haven't guessed by now it is all about your money, put a lock on your wallet.

d. Make sure your retirement money if it still there is not being used against you. Insist the local union, or government change the Erisa laws so that you or your community keep the loans local and the money local. Better still insist that the people taking your money and investing it in wall street invest it locally to produce jobs and green technology. I hate to say it but unions are heavy investors in wall street. They should not be doing that. Tell to local union and city council they should be investing that money at home. There are no interest rates increases for the foreseeable future anyway. If they had done that at Katrina or in the BP Oil spill the problems would have a solution, a local solution, local funds, money invested at home to directly benefit the communities where those funds came from in the first place. And don't forget to help local poor communities. If you don't' the poor and formerly middle class will be on the streets knocking at your door looking to feed their families too.

These are actions you can do; you can control and would be effective.

Tomorow: What to do about all those politicians and parties which also want your cash?

Update: August 12, 2010

So are things better yet? Sadly, no. But if only a few hundred thousand Americans followed the above advice change would occur. Wall Street and the Banks would feel that pinch, so tight is the system, that a few billion would likely threaten their bloated money needs. And, they would scramble in the next year or two to get money from the feds, like before, or up their fees. But, we would be gone local with our money. So a trap can be laid and set.

Now, to be clear, this is the single best thing to do to change things--re-direct your money locally.

Secondly, I am asked are Republicans better than Democrats since the former support local control. (Big laughter here) These Republicans are not talking about local control and self-sufficiency in my meaning. They are talking about their local control over you and your money. They are the same folks in bed with the Banks and Wall street. Are the Democrats better? Nope. We have to stop drinking the cool aid which makes us fail to see that they are all in it together, spending our money and squandering the future of our children. Go to the mirror and slap yourself three times and say "I must not think that the future lies with giving my money to any politician, Banker, or Wall street." (Yes Virginia Wall street counts on getting your unemployment check deposited regularly) So you are the golden goose.

Stop getting et.

So let us think on these things for the future.

Tomorow I outline Plan C. Plans A and B have been outlined above but we need too, a Plan C.

Sept 27, 2010

Here at the brink of the next election, what to do you may ask. The answer is clear; talk to local townspeople about implementing the above. Start a local dollar pool and co-op (like a local investment club) and meet in homes to get it started. The election is important. I won't tell you who to vote for because all of that is less important than taking control of our own future.

So what you may ask is plan C?

The first step is to make an analysis of what resources are available in your community to do the things outlined above, available land for self-sufficiency uses, available local capital, technical investment capital, available labor pools, political strategies, union supports for withdrawing money form banks and wall street and insisting that it be invested locally.

Investigate the Community Reinvestment Act and apply for funds for your community--which is the purpose of that act in the first place and billions are available. (These funds come directly from the Federal Reserve.)

Identify the goal as "Local Investment with Local Funds" and call a meeting to discuss the problems and local steps for your community while also seeking outside funds to aid in the development of those local institutions which will be needed.

You want in the end local foodstuffs, locally grown, local financing, and local labor and energy sources. You can do it in a city but it is difficult. (We all should look at how successful Detroit is in this.) But movement toward self-sufficiency is a good goal for every town, no matter to what degree that might be possible.

You probably have some ideas of your own, if you think about it.

Let's talk again later this week.

October 21, 2010

What can be done is to tell city hall to take the money out of the major banks and invest it locally or demand that the major banks invest it locally and that all mortgages be retained locally, We here are talking billions of dollars. The same should be said to the labor unions. What are they doing sending our money to Wall Street anyway? That worked our real well didn't it? It's our money; we should take steps to control how it is spent.

Now, the state: Letters and emails should go out to state governments to add stipulations to Wall Street investment contracts that state funds be invested in the state or at least that state generated dollars have a portion reinvested in the state. This already exists with banks in the Community Reinvestment Act and has been in place for years. Its precepts should be expanded and extended.

This is very doable. A companion piece ought to be to put a referendum in place which places these ideas before the state and have them embedded in law. If done, I guarantee you that the banks will do modifications and promote jobs and this country will move toward a sustainable recovery. It is your money. Don't give it away every payroll deduction and check to those who can't be trusted to protect middle class interests.

This is possible.

October 22, 2010

Now I have several emails asking how this re-distribution of banking dollars will actually work. The answer, I think, lies in the German example. Germany will, this year, post a 3 percent growth in GNP (Gross National Product) and will likely loan 150 billion to bail out Greece. Germany has bounced back from the recession and is doing well.

Why is this?

The main reasons are, in my view, lies with the German community banking system where communities directly invest in local banks and in many cases, own them. A second factor is that German workers, their middle class, sit on the boards of many corporations. A third factor is that the Germans did not decimate their manufacturing base the way other countries did. Finally, Germans save and hoard cash. It is their cultural way.

Add these factors together and what we have seen is that despite the near collapse of the German National Banking system and a German TARP of billions paid out by German taxpayers to save the National Banks, Germany has come through that just fine.

The reason is, I believe, are the factors identified above. We can do this in this country. Community banking, local investment, aligned with some of the other suggestions I have made above will work, if perused vigorously, But that is a big if.

Let us hope.

How to get our money back

http://www.authorsden.com/visit/viewshortstory.asp?id=53990&authorid=121255

How Does the Middle Class Get Back What Was Taken From it by the Banks?

Updated: Bank Transfer Day and Greece is being Foreclosed On. What is going on and how will it affect Americans? 11-6-11

In another blog on this site I have addressed the issue of dumping the big banks and have recommended that citizens take their money out of these large predatory banks and put them into municipal banks, state banks, credit unions, coops and the like.

In this way our economy becomes sup portative of local jobs, local communities and reverses the concentration of the last thirty years.

This will work and will work fairly quickly.

The big banks will try to kill this movement because it directly threatens the source of their power--our money.

Amazingly, Americans every day send virtually every dime they have, pension money, paycheck, savings, checking, city and state taxes--and deposit these monies into these few large predatory banks thereby

giving them the source of their power--our money. This is what must be stopped.

Thirty-eight percent of our 13 trillion dollar economy (five trillion) goes to Wall Street each year. Amazing.

30 years ago it was only 12 percent. Today we have become a finance- dominated economy where our own money has been used to dominate our lives-where wall street produces nothing and gets rich.

But taking money out of the predatory banks is only the first step.

There is more work to be done.

The next step is getting back the money stolen from tax payers.

Note: we are still poor even if we change banks.

We next have to take steps to retrieve the money Wall Street has in its vaults.

But, how to do that?

This is to be our ultimate goal-don't let the banks keep our money-otherwise not much has changed.

Here is what has to be done:

1-Have the loan principal on all home mortgages be written down to the current market values of those homes, and cease and desist on all home foreclosures.

This keeps people in their homes, provides dollar stimulus to the economy, reclaims neighborhoods blighted by foreclosures and gives the middle class a fighting chance to survive.

It also amounts to a refund of money stolen from these home owners and tax payers. The value of this rebate is about 6 trillion.

2-Tax capital gains and speculators and hedge fund profits at 15%.
These monies should go to fund jobs, education, infrastructure and social needs. This would produce 3.25 trillion dollars. This taxation rate is actually low compared to the 21-32 percent tax rate most of us pay. And to boot many corporations don't pay any taxes. Among the ones who pay that rate they average only 18% since they shelter their profits overseas and invest there in acts which border on economic treason. Americans love their country but tolerate this kind of disloyalty among the wealthy.

3-Increase the social security taxes on those with incomes over 117k. Why should these people not pay social security taxes above this income? This is the current situation. This would realize about 450 billion dollars.

4-Increase taxes on speculators and hedge-fund managers who currently control about 600 trillion dollars with no taxes, and no regulation. This is the famous hidden derivatives market. Yes, not taxed and not regulated. There are two banking systems in the world, the one we know about and the shadow banking system run by the central banks of the world.

The enormity of this becomes apparent when you realize that the global GNP for all countries today is only about 70 trillion per year.

You ask then how can there be 600 trillion in these hedge funds? The answer is that this is the leverage-debt bubble-derivatives spliced up fraudulently where the same mortgage is sold and resold, many to the European Banks, which is why we had to give them money from the Federal Reserve; which is partially why Europe's big banks are in trouble now. We sold them worthless derivatives and had to reimburse them.

But also in this unregulated market in order to purchase stock, options and puts, derivatives, and reinsurance schemes you only have to put 10% down or so. And note these huge wall street firms are using our money to make these bets-our money meaning that paycheck you deposited today and our money in the form of tax subsidies.

These hedge funds, banks, wall street and the federal reserve itself are leveraged to this incredible 600 trillion amount. It is the amount in the kitty owed but not yet paid for and/or worthless derivative stocks.

Banks are 40 to one debt to assets; the Federal Reserve is 60-to one. These hedge funds are essentially debt mills operating in the hundreds of trillions of dollars and all this is totally uncontrolled.

They have borrowed the money (using our money for collateral) to make wild investments in derivatives, third world ventures and in the IMF and the World Bank and in gold. And the rest is paper debt.

But most of the 600 trillion is toxic derivative investments

which are backed by nothing at all, and will collapse--
unless the central banks decide to print paper money which
in turn will result in massive inflation. Best to get our
money out before that occurs.

5-Default: Yes, default, There is not enough money in
circulation in all the world to pay 600 trillion. The amount
of paper money in circulation in the United States is only
about 3.3 trillion.

Imagine. This means that there is not enough money in the
whole country to pay the bills even if we had the money.
The rest of the 13 trillion in our economy is in debt, created
solely by computers. (Remember banks manufacture debt
money each time we make a loan. There is no actual
dollars backing this up. (See my blog on banks and how
they create money in a gigantic Ponzi scheme.)

So, it is inevitable debts will have to be written down
and/or not paid. The banks know this.

They know these loans can never be repaid even if we try;
all that will occur is that we become indentured debt slaves-
working all our lives to pay a debt which is structured such
that it can never be fully repaid.

Banks and countries on the other hand default all the time,
or they declare bankruptucy (General Motors?) But note the
terrible fact is that banks don't really have our money, it is
loaned out or exists in debt they owe and can't pay
(derivatives.)

But we lowly citizens are taught that debts are sacred
obligations and must be paid, while banks owe us and will
simply default on us closing their doors. This is no idle
claim. It happened in the 70's with the savings and loan

debacle when thousands of people lost their savings and over 1,500 bankers went to jail. But none today. Why is that?

Most of us anyway simply don't have the money to pay the banks   Wall Street and the usurious interest rates they now enforce.

All of this will likely then cause many of the large banks to crash.

So be it. My advice though is to get your money out of the large banks first because the huge wall street banking structure is not sustainable. Smaller banks will survive.

Besides we need a decentralized banking structure which, if we move our money, will be in place to replace the crooked banks on Wall Street.

The summary point is that it is not enough to stop the banks from stealing our money-we need to get the stolen money back in order for the middle class to survive--the middle class needs those funds.

I will have more tomorrow with more detail and additional ideas.

Sometimes the times require straight talk.

If none of the above is done, the middle class in this country will be impoverished for generations to come.

11-5-11
The "Move Your Money" movement and "Bank Transfer Day" are now launched. First word is that over 650,000 people have moved their accounts into credit unions and

the like and hundreds of thousands more have pledged to do so.

Saturday is not the best day to change banks, so next week the picture will become more clear.

The amount of money involved so far is about 4.5 billion dollars.

The implications of this include two big ones:

First 14 states are looking to create state banks.

California alone, if it did so, would bring on the domino effect among the large banks.

The banks then would run to the Federal Reserve (which is the chairs of all the big banks) and have more paper money created because they don't have California's money; it has been lost in derivative schemes or loaned out.

(So you see why I am advising the average citizen to get their money out.)

If not, when you get to the ATM it may happen that your card won't work.
The banks will declare a bank holiday, keep what money they have and declare a bank holiday and close permanently, with our money in their hands. It happened just this way in the crash of 1929.

This can happen: FDIC or no FDIC.

What most people don't know is that the FDIC is tax-payers money and the US doesn't have the money to give to the banks in this kind of scenario, and additionally, the United

States government does not control money.
The big predatory banks do via the Federal Reserve Bank.
They are the Federal Reserve.

So there will be no FDIC rescue in this situation especially since the budget of the FDIC is paid by the same large banks under discussion here. They will not fund an agency which under these conditions, participates in their own demise and who will be collecting from a closed bank? No one.

Chaos here.

It all could be brought on also by the fall of Greece via the domino effect.
ECM and American banks are the ones who bought many of these Greek bonds, the same ones which will not likely be repaid.

Yes, we are on the hook for Greece too-since our Federal Reserve loaned trillions to these European banks and they used some of that to buy Greece debt. So we are involved if these banks do not pay us back, which is the case, since a deal has been struck where Greece has had 50 percent of its debt forgiven. That affects us and our bank will have to take the haircut as well. That is why all of the governments and banks have joined together to make the populations involved take the austerity, so that they, the banks, don't have to take profit losses.

Now the European Common Market is looking for money from China at least two trillion, but that will not be enough even if they get it because Greece is a small country with a small debt (320 billion) compared to Italy and Spain. These latter two are in trouble as well and there is nothing this side of heaven that the ECM can do to save those two countries.

Their debts are astronomical-eight times those of Greece.
Italy alone has debt in the trillions.

So you see trouble looms here.

We are now seeing Greece auctioned off, their water, their
factories, their schools, their monuments are all to be sold
to private investors (American hedge fund people and the
central banks) as a way of paying off the Greek debt-this In
addition to lower wages, no health care, and
impoverishment of their middle class.

That is why there are riots in the streets. An entire country
is being sold to these "investors" who are using our money
to get rich literally buying up Greece. Their young people
are leaving the country in droves--no jobs and no income.

This has happened for years to third world countries but
this is the first set European countries including Ireland and
Iceland to literally be taken over by the predatory hedge
funds and the predatory banks.

So countries are being treated just like the average citizen;
Greece is being foreclosed on.

How will all this end? More: tomorrow, a few suggestions,
as to the way out of the mess.

The Middle Class, The Poor and America's Future

This essay looks at why American politics has the contours that it exhibits. It asks the question what political stances do the poor, the middle class and the rich take in our political system and why.
Second, a comparison with European political systems is made looking at these same class groups and the similarities and differences we see there and why.

The Middle Class Holocaust Coming:

In the recent mid-term elections in the United States political debate excluded two enormous topics of obvious import: the two wars in Iraq and Afghanistan and the plight of the poor and middle classes in the United States.

The economy was discussed but not its real impacts on real people now short of resources and whose life chances are declining. Rather, we were treated to debates about tax cuts, deficit reductions, "big government" and "socialism."

Why should these discussions take on these contours?

We will have a look at the middle classes and the working poor in the American political landscape and how they place themselves in the political spectrum and why.

We shall also compare that to the multi-party system and the coalition patterns extent in Europe. There we find distinctly different political patterns and outcomes: we ask how do these two systems compare and why and with what political outcomes.

Let's start with a quote from two European scholars who ask the questions; do political coalitions between the middle class and the working poor explain the nature of political structures in Europe? Why are there no coalitions between the poor and the middle class in the United States?

The scholars Iversen and Soskice are quoted from a paper given by Phillip Manow in Seoul, Korea in March of 2007 gives us some clues as to why such coalitions exist in Europe but not in the United States. See link below.

http://www.korea.ac.kr/~kwon/Conf/Manow.pdf

Here is a longish quote from that paper.

"Iversen and Soskice start from the basic observation that in multi-party systems the left is in government more often whereas the right more often governs in two-party systems. Why is this so?

In a multi-party system the lower and the middle classes together can tax the rich and share the revenue. In a two party system the middle class can either vote for a Centre-left party or a Centre-right party. If the left governs, the middle class has to fear that the left government will tax both the upper and the middle class for the exclusive benefit of the lower class. If a right party governs, the middle and upper class will not be taxed and redistribution will be marginal. Therefore, in a two-party system the middle class has the choice either to be taxed and to receive no benefits, or not to be taxed and to receive no benefits. Obviously, it would prefer then not to be taxed.

From this simple and highly stylized account it is clear that the middle class will more often vote together with the lower class in multi-party systems – or to be more precise:

middle class parties will more often enter into coalitions with lower class parties in multi-party systems than in two party systems.2"

Underlying this analysis is a stark premise: Politics is about money and resources--who gets what, when, where and how.

Another premise, equally important and less apparent, seems to be that prosperity must be shared for a culture to flourish. A peaceful means to accomplish this must be identified and institutionalized. Otherwise, the rich will greedily absorb a disproportionate share of everything, refuse to give it up, and the society ultimately is thrown into riots, anger, social dislocations, revolution and all things bad and not so incidentally, the destruction of the middle class.

Well lets see how these principles do and do not apply to America, especially since at this critical juncture, these are precisely the questions which our country now confronts, even as political discourse ignores them altogether--if we take the last election as an indicator.

Next time. Who is getting what, when, where, why, and how in the United States.

Nov 29, 2010

I make the argument that the systematic attack on the middle class in this country involving so-called deficit cut backs, privatizing social security, cutting Medicare, cutting education spending, cutting wages, contemplating millions of unemployed indefinitely, also constitute opportunities. There are now opportunities for the middle class, in seeing itself becoming lower middle class, to begin to see and form a coalition with the working poor classes and to see it has common interests with even the current poor.

From this an ethos of common prosperity can emerge and the country can get back on the right track again.

Having most wealth the hands of the rich is an unsustainable idea.

This opportunity for the middle class to finally see that all the money in this country is money they themselves supply to Wall Street institutions who translate those funds into political power which has been used to ransack that very same middle class--taking from them in just three years, their home values, their savings, their jobs--and their futures even unto retirement--all under the guise of deficit reduction. This is a middle class holocaust.

This is and will become even more devastating. It in fact, it turns America into a true welfare state: The rich controlling most wealth in a Neo-Dickens world where most will have to depend upon alms from a government controlled by those very same rich classes.

http://www.nytimes.com/2010/12/05/us/politics/05states.html?ref=todayspaper

Fish are having trouble identifying water.
More tomorrow: where we will focus on "deficit reduction" and the agenda behind it.

Dec 4, 2010
Actually, I started another blog on deficit reduction on this site. Refer to that blog.

The Alternatives to the Big Banks

The American Public is fed up and looking for alternatives to big banks. Below are a few ideas being put forward.

If we are fed up with the big banks what are the alternatives?

Surprisingly there is a lot of material on this topic with many different alternatives being put forward.

Below are several links which explore ideas in this area.

But first know that Nov 5th has been designated "Bank Transfer Day" where the Occupy Wall Street folks and other Americans plan to march to the local giant predatory bank and withdrawn their funds.

But where to put those funds once they have been withdrawn?

But first see the links below:

on the "Bank Transfer Day."

on how to close out your bank account -a guide.

on the various kinds of non-profit banks and calls for state and community banks-even to break up the big banks.

on new ways to finance local communities and local merchants-not allowing Wall Street to finance Walmarts of the world who come in and drive local merchants out of business.

Finally there is a link to a radio show which documents the deliberate plan to destroy this country financially, by a former Bush Administration official.

Then tomorrow we go over the detail and I make suggestions.

Here are those links:

The Credit Unions prepare for all the new customers on Bank Transfer Day
http://www.cutimes.com/2011/10/28/bank-transfer-day-community-banks-cus-gear-up
A Nation-wide Movement to Install Local, State and Community banks:
http://www.yesmagazine.org/people-power/occupy-the-banks-strategies-for-transformation

How to Close Out Your Account at the Big Predatory Bank:
http://www.yesmagazine.org/new-economy/a-field-guide-to-closing-your-bank-account

New Ways to Finance a Come-back for Local Communities:
http://www.yesmagazine.org/issues/the-new-economy/new-economy-new-ways-to-do-finance

Interview with Former Bush Administration Official Who Tells All
http://www.kpfa.org/archive/id/74534

7/8/13

 How the big banks are moving to kill credit union competition.

http://www.truth-out.org/buzzflash/commentary/item/18073-monopolistic-too-big-to-fail-banks-try-to-crush-credit-unions-as-competition-by-removing-tax-exemption

Taxes, Deficits and Elections

Here we go. There will be no turns in Washington for the next two years because noses will be growing longer and longer.
Updated: Nov 5, 2010-"There Will Be No Jobs Soon"
Update: Nov 6, 2010 "Now Let Me Get This Straight--Give 600 Billion to the Banks?" Who Thought This Was A Good Idea?
Update: Dec 2, 2010 Bullocks Anyone?

November 3, 2010

Here we are the day after the elections and the pundits are out in force spinning the results. The Republicans are planning a January trip to Washington to put an end to debt, government spending, the health care bill, and all things Obama.

The Democrats are pointing to silver linings, doing "mi culpa" and basically saying that "we did some good things" but secretly happy that they don't have to take heat before the 2012 presidential election when the big money gets back in play.

This is not to minimize the results of the elections for both, but the fact remains that both sides have sold out to wall-street, the banks, and the corporations.

So nothing will change except the increasing impoverishment of the middle classes, a deepening recession, unto a depression, huge banks playing blackjack with depositor's money and a volatile angry, American politics where little is actually accomplished; thereby maintaining an entrenchment of the status quo. And this is precisely the outcome which benefits Wall Street.

No change or loans for us thank you very much.

The banks are taking our money, (add to this 600 billion from the Federal Reserve) and using it to cover their own toxic assets, increase our debt to them, and trying to reduce the value of the dollar to raid the central banks of other countries, buy up their real estate and other assets with these cheaper dollars. It will ignite a currency war.

But meantime back home, here are a few important items of note which will have an immediate impact in the next few months.

Let's see what the deeper meanings underlie, not only the election, but the next 60 days.

1-This election essentially involved the loss of 35 or so blue dog democrat seats in mostly red states. Therefore, there is a resetting the clock back to the pre-Obama period. These blue dog democrats were way right of the center of the party and now what has occurred is the democrats have a much more left party caucus pressing Obama from the left. There will be fewer moderate republicans to please, because they are gone from the party so now there is a clarification of the battle lines for 2012.

Moreover, since 55% of the electorate did not show up for these mid-terms, things will look very different when the mass of these voters show up in that presidential year in 2012. Both parties know this and the next two years are a waiting period as they both try to appear busy.

2- Secondly the Tea-Party people will, even before January, have to witness the current republican establishment face several critical dilemmas:

A. The Federal Debt ceiling has expired. The current Republicans have to decide whether to let the government come to a halt, ala Newt Gingrich in 1994, and risk immediate public anger and probably face Tea-Party pressure to let it happen. They will, if unwise, let the ceiling expire and government come to a halt pretending they are the new more tea-party Republican Party and to hell with the public; they look conservative and responsible.

They could decide to extend last year's budget which would require no debt ceiling legislation; or increase the debt limit of the republic, up to perhaps over 15 trillion dollars-this would have to be done by early spring--or do it with some fancy accounting tricks, or they could steal the money from the social security trust fund which they have done in the past to pay for wars.

But these are unavoidable dilemmas, so expect an avoidance in an off the books accounting gambit to hide an increase in the debt ceiling.

What will also likely happen is an extension of the current budget until after January when the Tea-Party people show up. But they will show up angry because the Republican establishment essentially voted to keep the current deficit budget and spending going.

The current Republican establishment could whack off huge chunks of the current budget in the next 60 days (not likely) like social security, the pentagon budget, health care, the poor; but where would such cuts come from in the amount of money to make a real difference? No where, that's where. Expect a freeze to keep up appearances.

Also, if possible, expect the Republicans to punt to the Tea-Party people who come in January--if they cannot get Obama to join with them in a secret pact agreement about what to cut.

3-Then there are the Bush Tax Cuts which expire December 31, 2010. What to do about that? Ignore it, extend the deadline, or cut a deal with Obama to have all tax cuts extended?

At issue here is that among the tax cuts is the Alternative Minimum Tax cuts which benefit the middle class. If the cuts are not extended it will end that tax cut for the middle classes who will scream bloody murder, even as they might like to see the tax cuts for the rich expire.

Complicated, huh?

So you can see what the horse-trading is likely to be. My prediction: all tax cuts will be extended--the Democrats to protect the middle class and the Republicans to protect the rich.

Then there is the health care bill and its implementation aspects, some of which have to be decided in committee. This is ugly, but any hearings will also make it clear that the bill has lot in it which benefits the middle class and to air that would help the democrats and Obama. So we will see a lot of general talk, seeking to keep resentment going, but few real changes.

And then there is the unemployment extension for the 99 month people. Congress left town without doing anything about that and the deadline to do so is here in November. December is urgent. If they don't act you'll have a chunk of people upset, and unemployed for the holidays; not to mention the loss of consumer purchasing power to help the economy recover. The Republicans and TP people will have to wear Scrooge Hats around Christmas time if they don't act.

The Economy: Here we are at the economy. What can the Dems and Reps do about the economy in the next sixty days? Not much. The ideological lines of demarcation are so rigid there is little room for compromise. The Dems will claim slow progress and the Reps will claim the Dems made the unemployment mess and both of their noses will grow longer and longer.

Finally, to boot, the Tea-Party people will be looking over Republican shoulders in the next 60 days making their views known about what to do about the above items, and being ideological purists that they are, they will come to town angry no matter what the Republican establishment types do.

So the scene is set.

So what is likely to happen in the next two years? The Republicans will overplay their hands and subpoena everyone, threaten to shut down the government, back off of massive cuts, especially in the military (too many republican votes there, back off social security, too many republican votes there etc.) all the while claiming massive victories for the benefit of the back home crowd.

In the end only Wall-street and the banks will in fact, be left standing dusting off their checkbooks for the 2012 elections to make sure that nothing in Washington changes- once again.

This blog is not for the faint of heart.

Nov. 5, 2010

Just note here to be amplified upon tomorrow. All the talk today is of the economy and of jobs.
The truth is that "putting America back to work" is a flawed strategy. Think of it this way. At the present rate of job accretion, it will take five to fifteen years to recover the 11 million jobs lost since the recession began.

It will not happen. It takes a100 thousand jobs a month just to keep pace with population growth and 150 thousand jobs a month is minor compared to the need.

Add to this the fact that the long term unemployed are not employable and may have to be given re-training which will cost billions we don't have. Add this to the returning vets who need jobs, housing etc. whose medical costs are high in an already aging population; add to this that many of the jobs created are low-paying service jobs and you have a bleak outlook on jobs.

Jobs will not happen- and that is the real problem-- especially if you understand the real unemployment and underemployment rate is 17%.

So what to do? For a short answer see my blog on this site on "A Report Card On Obama" and a companion blog on this site called "What America Needs to do to Survive." See the Nov 5th entry where this discussion begins.

More detail tomorrow.

Nov 6, 2010

Obama and company recognize the fact that jobs will not be coming back. So what to do while pretending that they will?

The current strategy apparently is to float the 600 billion onto the currency market, allowing the dollar to dip in value, thereby, increasing the demand for cheaper American goods and thereby increase American exports and thereby increase American jobs.

Sound convoluted?

Well that's because it is.

The announcement that his trip to India (now underway) with 200 American tycoons in tow, will result in 50 thousand new jobs is to put window dressing on the problem. Yet, true , it is a start.

What has to be done I have identified in Obama blog on this site.

The problem is simple:
Consumers, who propel 70% of the American economy, are debt ridden, and like good soldiers some are trying to pay down the Debt That Has No End. They will default in increasingly massive numbers. (Already happening.)
What has to be done is to lower or forgive that debt or put money in their pockets by direct dollars--that would have been a better use of the 600 billion-- rather than the round-about-give-to-the-banks-first strategy. They will simply spend it over seas and not put a dime into America.

Gloomy? Well yes. But not if people take off the blinders and see what is occurring. Things have changed. What we do, therefore, has to change also.

The old strategies will not work.
So we have to look to new ones.

I have a few, modest suggestions. Tomorrow.

Dec 2, 2010

Time is short today so first lets list some solutions and come back tomorrow for the detail.

1-The military budget is 60% of the total federal budget. It has to be cut because that is where the money is. 10% cut = 100 billion

2-The top 1% of the population has 35% of the wealth and half the tax rates of the rest of us. Tax their stock market holdings 15% along with capital and dividend income. 15% revenue= 1.8 trillion

3- Increase the current cap on social security and Medicare taxes to include the wealthy. The current system has no tax on people earning above 110k per year and is a free ride for the wealthy. Best guess is 2.3 billion inflow.

4-Have a tax payroll holiday for the middle classes thereby putting money in their pocket, increase the home mortgage deduction, and declare a moratorium on foreclosures. Outflow approximately 2 trillion.

5-Put the 600 billion into mortgage relief, greening and insulating American homes. Remember winter is coming and oil prices are rising. There will be demand to keep warm. It will be a long winter with high prices and cold voters, otherwise. Dollar return on this investment is two dollars for every dollar invested =1.2 trillion

That is the flavor of some of the suggestions and any three of them will eliminate the so-called deficit. (Net of all of them is 1.3 trillion against a deficit of 1.2 trillion. No more deficits.

There is no need to go after social security. That program has no deficit.
No need to go after the middle class at all.
The money on Wall Street is our money and they should have to give it back.

These are just preliminary but achievable in a short period of time, absent political stagnation. I know that is a big if, but a solution is a solution even if blocked.

Let's hope our leaders get some bull apparatus and act.

A look at the facts and myths about:
Social Security-is the fund going broke?
Medicare: Will Its Cost Bankrupt Us?
The Military Budget: Is It Really 60% of the Total Budget?
Social Programs: How Much Do They Really Cost?
Deficit: What Is To Be Done?

Updated: 12/20/13 Deficit: Up or Down? The Facts: What the press doesn't tell you.

Updated: 9/11/12 What will be the triggers and events which can cause a financial crisis-worldwide?

Updated: 9/8/12 Jobs, why are there no jobs and what to do?

Updated: 9/4/12 Who has looted America and how?

Updated: 9/2/12 What are the details of the current debt and who really caused it?

Updated 11-30-10-So Where Is The Money?

Updated 12-1-10 "If You Want Money for the Deficit, You Have To Go Where the Money Is."

Dec 3, 2010 "Now Let me get this straight: My pension will help fund the European Bailout of Ireland, Greece, Spain?

Dec 10, 2010 So who is going to be taxed again?

In this blog I was just trying to find out the facts about these items in a period where "deficit-cutting" and "big government" blare out of my TV, the pages in the press, and among friends who opine right and left on these matters.

So I thought I would do a little investigation myself. In the coming few days I will share with you what I found out.

MYTH: Social Security is causing part of our deficit and is going broke.

FACTS: First a quote from a New York Times article from the chief actuary manager of the fund (Mr. Goss) and a second quote from the Director of the Congressional Office of the Budget.

Mr. Goss is talking about the state of fund based on 2009 figures and projections and the proceeds from the funds' investments in treasury securities.

"In a year like this, the paper gains from the interest earned on the securities will more than cover the difference between what it takes in and pays out."

'Mr. Goss, the actuary, emphasized that even the $29 billion shortfall projected for this year was small, relative to the roughly $700 billion that would flow in and out of the system. The system, he added, has a balance of about $2.5 trillion that will take decades to deplete. Mr. Goss said that large cushion could start to grow again if the economy recovers briskly.'

'Indeed, the Congressional Budget Office's projection shows the ravages of the recession easing in the next few years, with small surpluses reappearing briefly in 2014 and 2015.'

See the link below for the full article.

http://www.nytimes.com/2010/03/25/business/economy/25social.html

For those who are numbers junkies, like myself, should also take a look an article which details the Federal Budget for 2010, and for 2011. See link below:
http://topics.nytimes.com/top/reference/timestopics/subject

s/f/federal_budget_us/index.html?inline=nyt-classifier

The Deficit Commission Plan comes out December 1, 2010 and is not likely to have the 14 votes necessary for a vote in the House of Representatives. Meantime, many groups have their own ideas for deficit management. Here is a link detailing some of those plans. We will then evaluate the whole lot afterward. Meantime a link:

http://www.nytimes.com/2010/11/29/us/politics/29fiscal.html?_r=1&ref=federal_budget_us

Home work.

Come back tomorrow and we will begin to sort all of this out.

Nov 30, 2010

Truth Telling About Social Security

First the question is does Social Security contribute to the deficit?

Answer no.

The program has a 2.5 trillion dollar surplus at the present time. So why would the Deficit commission target one of the few programs which has a surplus and money available to operate out to 2037?

It makes no sense. So why is it on the chopping block?

Well, first let us have a look at where this tremendous surplus money comes from.

Answer:

It comes from you and I. Every pay check a sum is deducted from our paychecks for our social security retirement and those funds are placed in the social security trust fund and much of it is invested with the idea of increasing its total amount so that it will be there when we are ready to retire. That is the story put out there. But it is true ?

So, like good investigators we want to know the truth and to find out the truth in America you have to follow the prime rule of thumb:

Follow the money because there lays the truth.

The truth is that the 2.5 trillion has been raided by the federal government, mainly to pay for wars the country could not afford (remember Iraq and Afghanistan?) for bank bailouts, (remember, instituting the Bush Tax Cuts which we could not afford?) Remember the lost jobs, the lost manufacturing base; the Wall-Street bail outs?

How can a country afford all of this in a little less than a decade?

Answer: We, the people, could afford it because we saved up each month.

But the money was taken from yours and my retirement funds, social security monies, yours and my pension funds (remember we are also putting money in that pot too, yours and my taxes, yours and my daily deposits in the banks, yours and my Medicare taxes, yours and my unemployment funds, at an actual taxation rate of 53%--all this ultimately ending up in the hands of the banks, the corporations, and wall street who were taxed at 16% and was used by them to generate obscene profits overseas and/or obscene losses which ended up having to be paid for by raiding our retirement funds to cover such losses and monies wasted in endless and permanent wars and other boondoggles.

I don't mind government spending, at least you get something back for that money after the monied classes have deducted their deductions, loop holes and subsidies benefits which, while only a pittance, is better than the alternatives of no benefits at all.

But what did we get back for the purloining of our money by the corporations--jobs and profits exported overseas. What did we get back for the purloining of our money by wall street--economic collapse and bank gambling, lost values in our homes, in our 401k.s, almost permanent unemployment, and now a threat to our pension funds (remember this is our money too, deducted every paycheck,) low or no pensions, foreclosures, impossible credit card debt and to boot, in all this, we are told it is our fault and we have to learn to tighten our belts.

I don't know about you but this doesn't seem right.

Well that is because it isn't.

More tomorrow.

First: a glance at borrowing from the Social Security Fund, since 2002. This borrowing was clearly seen coming and predicted. Here is one prediction. After we will see if the prediction came true .But first the prediction:

1998: Testimony by Alan Greenspan with Senator Hollings
saying:
"We owe Social Security 736 billion right this minute."

In 2002 actual borrowing from the fund: 165.4 billion
2003-projected--164 billion
2004-projected--180.6 billion
2005-projected--203.8 billion
2006-projected--226.1 billion
2007-projected--247.9 billion
2008-projected--268. billion

Total projected borrowing: 1.11 trillion from the fund.

Source:

http://demopedia.democraticunderground.com/discuss/dubo
ard.php?az=show_mesg&forum=102&topic_id=17321&m
esg_id=18550

Now how much did we actually borrow and how much
exactly is left in the fund in cash. (Actual income for the
social security trust fund in 2009 was about 700 billion and
outlays are about 520 billion.)

And what about the unemployment trust fund. What is the
story there?

That tomorrow.

But the point is that someone here loses big, because the
banks, the government, the corporations got the money and
can't or won't pay it back to us and therefore all of the talk
about cutting social security. Why: because the funds on
paper are 2.5 trillion but some of that the cash is long gone
and what is left in the fund is a lot of IOU's-to us and the

banks and wall street can't or don't want to pay it back.

But exactly, again, how much real cash is left for the boomers you and I?

It difficult to find out this piece of information.

What does all this mean and what is to be done?

Hint: There are solutions.

Hint: You can't look at a government debt and a government budget like the family budget. It is not like the family budget. Don't fall for that false analogy.
In our family budget we cannot print money in the basement--the government can (or more accurately, the Federal Reserve, the banks can;) we cannot raid our neighbors for resources, the government and our banks can.

We can't create taxes. The government can.

Well, you get the idea. There is no real analogy between one's home budget and the processes which underlie the budget of an entire country. So ignore politicians we try to tell you they are the same. They are not.

So what then you ask is to be done?

Tomorrow.

December 1, 2010

Busy day today so lets cut to the chase and identify what will really cure the deficit. We will post here an outline and in the coming days go to detail on some of them.

But first what will not work:

1-Cutting down the middle class and driving it to poverty will not work obviously and will likely in a year or two create a huge rebellion once people realize what has happened to them. A likely trigger will be the Republican discussion of eliminating the home mortgage deduction. This will do it. Not only have Americans seen their homes lose 40% value but the elimination of that deduction will increase their taxes by thousands of dollars, and put even old ladies in the streets in outrage.

Moreover, the consequences of this kind of action will be:

Lower revenues (taxes) for states, cities and localities, lower purchasing power for an economy which is 70% middle class consumer driven; higher defaults, foreclosures, rising health care costs because people will drop health insurance and flood the emergency rooms for health care.
Impoverishing the middle class, therefore, is not a good idea and helps no one.

2-Cutting back government spending or attacking the deficit in dollar amounts large enough to make a difference, is a pipe dream.

You might as well shut down the entire government, and move us all to third world status. Government spending is the one area that the middle class gets something back for its taxes.
We get nothing back from the banks and wall street,. We, not them, fuel the economy of this country. 70% of the GNP comes from the middle classes and we pay the taxes-- yet the profits go to the banks and Wall Street and the

corporations. **The middle class provides the only real money in the entire system.**

The rest of the institutions in the United States suck on that teat.

3-Cutting the military budget substantially, while desirable and possible since we spend 60% of the government's budget on the military, the fact is that will take years to accomplish and since the military is so entwined in our economy it has become yet another institution too big to fail and so many Americans depend upon military largess to survive--but that budget has to be cut anyway, but it has to be done gradually and with perhaps an initial 10% cut to start things off. (This has already been proposed by Gates, but he wants to "re-invest" those savings back into the military, therefore, it is not a real cuts. I say let's take a real cut.)

4-Economic growth as a way of reducing or eliminating the deficit, (jobs and exports) is too slow to avoid disaster. We will all be in rags before the jobs return and that will take at least five years.

What can be done then? Let's start with a simple idea. There is not a shortage of money to be used to eliminate the deficit. The problem is that 35% of our money is in the hands of 1% of the population-the so-called market.

Solution: Get our money back.

I like Richard Woff's ideas about taking the income of all individuals with more than a million dollars invested in the stock market and apply an additional 15% tax rate. They keep 85% and this will eliminate the deficit over night. Really it would.

What is astounding is that the so-called deficit commission has not even brought this up. Why? The two chairs of the commission and most members of that commission represent those same wall-street-banks interests. So no surprise this is not included in possible solutions. (See Richard Wolff's ideas on this)

The mess wall-street has made we are going to have to pay for while wall street proceeds forward, "fully recovered" from any of the effects of the recession and notice that every announcement that the unemployment rate has gone up is greeted by a rise on wall street. Why; because middle class assets become cheaper and the unemployed default and foreclosures become available cheap. Meantime the big bonus payments have returned.

The American people will catch on sooner or later to all of this and there will be hell to pay.

When you want to reduce or eliminate deficits at home or in government you have to go where the money and the money is in the hands of these monied classes who in the last thirty years have gotten rich off the rest of us and now it is time they pay that money back. They have gotten rich off the American credit card and our loans to them-(yes we loan them our money every time we make a deposit.)

But who are these folks and how much would be really made available if we did this?

More details tomorrow.

Dec 3, 2010

But the problem is not just an American problem. We are a part of the global finance system. Just out is the revelation that during the finance crisis of 2008 and continuing, the Federal Reserve Bank loaned over *9 trillion dollars* to itself, to banks foreign banks and domestic, to cover their losses.

That is 9 ***trillion dollars***, not counting the 600 billion now coming over the horizon!

Where did this money come from, remembering the entire yearly output of the American economy in one year is only 13 trillion?

For comparison a billion seconds is 32 years: a trillion seconds is 32,000 years. A trillion is a very large burrito.

Why did this happen and where did this 9 trillion dollars come from?

Answer: The banks used partly our funds, our pension monies, our daily deposits and the Fed simply printed the rest. Understand this is how the system works.

But the real news here is that the 9 trillion was essentially used to cover the fraudulent investments wall street had sold to investors foreign and domestic. A good part of it was to pay foreign banks back who might have collapsed once it was known that such investments were worthless. The US essentially had to take our money to cover up that fraud and lost gamble and our their selling fraudulent assets to these foreign banks.

Meantime, companies like Goldman Sachs, had seen this coming and essentially took out re-insurance and took short positions on all of this, even as they sold these worthless assets to others and reaped huge profits in doing so.

AIG the major re-insurer, Fanny and Freddie Mac, FDIC, the American tax payer took the losses, and the banks took the profits. This is welfare for the rich.

And the story does not end here.

The domino rolled right across the ocean to the European Common Market where the bail outs of Ireland, Greece, Portugal, and Spain now loom.

Austerity programs will not solve anything there.

In fact, the European Central Bank does not have the money for the bailouts, up to a trillion dollars, and will not have anything like what it will need if Italy goes belly up-- which it will.

In fact, the ECM will have to get part of the money it needs, not just from Germany and France or England, but from American taxpayers.

The Germans will give much but there is a limit since their taxpayers will revolt at some point if they are made to suffer to bail out others.

So how you ask will all this get done? It will get done by borrowing money from the managers of those huge pension funds which exist at the Federal, State and Local Level in the United States and elsewhere and the Federal Reserve buying ECM bonds. This, again, is our pension monies and deposit monies and the accumulated profits wall street has from the so-called recession.

The American taxpayer actually is helping to fund banks all over the world--foreign and domestic--with our pensions, taxes, social security funds, unemployment insurance funds etc.

This will be the second bubble to hit in 2012. All of this is not sustainable as currently constructed.

But the chief aspect of this which is not sustainable is that the profits cannot continue to be grabbed by the few. The entire system has to be re-constituted to produce prosperity for the many not just the few.

Actually, that is the European Common Market's underlying principle. The strong help the weak. We have to learn that trick here in the United States by ensuring that the strong don't use our money to prevent this bedrock principle of shared prosperity from being implemented, which they have succeeded in doing in the last 30 years.

Ok, now that you are cheered up there is a need for a hot toddy or something.

Tomorrow we go to detail.

December 10, 2010

Forgot to mention that the new tax deal is not so great. More detail on this next week but the facts are:

1-That the lowest earners have their taxes go up not down, or neutral

2- The longest term unemployed are left out of the deal entirely (the 99 month people)

3- The Estate Tax exempts those earning five and 10 million per couple, per year, thereby increasing the deficits of every state in the union.

4-Social security, unemployment, and disability incomes remain taxed. (This is double taxation, these earnings are taxed when taken out of our paychecks and taxed again when we use these funds. Note capital gains and dividend income remain taxes only at the 15% percent level while the rest of our income is taxed at the 21% level.

The democrats are right to revolt against job-killing tax breaks for the rich.

9/2/12

But, first a closer look at the deficit and debt.

World Debt-Who caused it-Who Got the Money-and Who has to pay it back?

The world we live in is a construction of the banks using phony debt as a means of control.

So let's have a look at the debt leader of the world -the United States. How did this happen? How did this debt happen?

First let's today settle the question of who or what caused the deficit in the United States in the first place such that the government had to borrow all that money and who got rich of the debt we currently have.

First a little history of debt in this country and then we go to the specifics.

http://www.authorsden.com/visit/viewarticle.asp?catid=23&id=62616

Turns out the greatest contributor to the greatest debt in US history was George Bush.

See below:

Debt increased from 133 billion to 1 trillion during his administration. This was the Republican "starve the beast" strategy--create a debt ridden government and then under the cover of austerity took back middle class assets, ignoring the fact that two wars made Republican defense contractors, the banks, , the pentagon, the so-called security industry and wall street--all rich.

There is no justice here.

On top of all this is the claim that the middle class overspent and now has to tighten its belt because the monied classes simultaneously reduced wages forcing the middle class to put their wives, children and grannies to work and use bank high interest rate credit cards to survive.

Why can't the American public see this scam is beyond me.

But a chart is worth a thousand words.

http://jimcgreevy.com/gvdc/Natl_Debt_Chart.html

It is clear that the Republicans ran up the debt with bailouts for banks, two wars, and tax breaks for the rich.

I am suggesting this was and is no accident.

And they are poised to do it again because there are billions in profits in it for their constituents-the banks, the pentagon, the so-called security industry, the prison industrial industry, and the war profiteers.

To be clear:

1. Banks, corporations and wall street love high unemployment- which means people are desperate and work for half wages-this has happened already.
2. They love recession because prices fall down drastically and since they have all of our money, have kicked us out of our homes, they have the cash and buy up these cheap homes themselves at half prices. Most foreclosed properties are bought by the banks themselves, since the down priced homes also now have lower taxes.

3- They love war since war profiteers get rich and to boot they have made many communities in the US dependent upon the local war industries dependent upon them and the Pentagon for jobs.

4. They love privatizing schools and have attacked the public school system, depriving the schools of revenue and tax money and then come in saying the schools are failing and should be privatized into "charter" schools.

5. They love drugs crime and fill up the jails with people of color in a new Jim Crow system and in addition provided jobs in rural communities run by private companies. The industrial prison complex is a jobs program for rural areas as well as billions for farmers--all republicans.

6. They make billions off school loans and the even the school lunch programs.

Their tentacles are everywhere, using OUR money to do it.

Tomorrow let's go back for more detail and a prognosis on the above which is clearly not sustainable. It will be a re-run of 1929. See the PBS video special on the 1929 debacle to get a look at how it all worked then.

http://www.pbs.org/wgbh/americanexperience/films/crash/

http://www.treasurydirect.gov/govt/resources/faq/faq_publ icdebt.htm#DebtOwner

9/3/12
US companies preparing for Greece to leave the Eurozone. Yes, they are.

http://www.nytimes.com/2012/09/03/business/economy/us-companies-prepare-in-case-greece-exits-euro.html?ref=business

"In a survey this summer, the firm found that 80 percent of clients polled expected Greece to leave the euro zone, and a fifth of those expected more countries to follow.

"Fifteen months ago when we started looking at this, we said it was unthinkable," said Heiner Leisten, a partner with the Boston Consulting Group in Cologne, Germany, who heads up its global insurance practice. "It's not impossible or unthinkable now."

Mr. Leisten's firm, as well as PricewaterhouseCoopers, has already considered the timing of a Greek withdrawal — for example, the news might hit on a Friday night, when global markets are closed.

A bank holiday could quickly follow, with the stock market and most local financial institutions shutting down, while new capital controls make it hard to move money in and out of the country."

Is this a likely scenario for the United States as well?

9/4/12

 Cal Pers pension fund underfunded by 50%. Pensioners have lost half of their life savings with zero interest rates.

http://www.youtube.com/watch?list=PL768846B770CB8C95&v=UgnqBOarHHw&feature=player_detailpage

More on the true causes of the deficit:

 http://www.huffingtonpost.com/2012/09/05/republican-party-deficit_n_1858295.html?ref=topbar#slide=1476568

 Half of the unemployed collect no unemployment benefits which most of them paid into for most of their working lives and have arbitrarily been cut off by Congress-all to provide, cheap, docile and willing labor for the corporations. Terrible.

http://www.nationofchange.org/half-america-s-unemployed-workers-are-collecting-no-unemployment-benefits-1347111689

Why have we not recovered? Here is a letter to the editor I happen to agree with from a small businessman.
Comment from:

http://www.nationofchange.org/jobs-report-and-election-1347110763

" JOBS REPORT & THE ELECTION: Month after month we all crowd around the TV set awaiting news of the employment trend, i.e., "Up" or "Down," all the while ignoring the most fundamental issue relating to employment numbers. Businesses that do not have access to financing cannot expand operations, and therefore, will not hire workers. The President can't merely wish jobs into existence. Job creation is directly related to the demand for goods/services and to supply of the financing necessary to deliver on this demand, opening new jobs positions. The banks were bailed-out. Period! Instead of doing the "right thing," making loans to entrepreneurs {Small Businesses} they chose, instead, to park the bail-out money in the bond market. While that action may have served to guarantee minimal revenue in the form of the interest payments collected, it does nothing to stimulate activity in the larger economy. I personally have been trying to open a business for the last 4 years. I have incorporated in a tax haven {Nevada} and have religiously filed my paper-work on time, have developed a new product prototype, {or rather an improvement on existing products} but could not get a loan. I have had to rely solely on savings from my job {despite two lay-offs of 18 months and 12 months respectively}. In spite of the uncertainty engendered by this state-of-affairs, I was able to save enough to cover the cost of my start-up... but it has taken nearly 5 years! Lack of access to capital has been the biggest drag on the economy that we live in. The "Tax Rate" has absolutely NOTHING to do with my decision to go into business, my ability to R

& D, nor the reasons why capital cannot be accessed to speed the process along. So much for the bogus argument that high taxes causing would-be small businesses not to go into business. That argument is complete and total B.S!!! Neither do regulations have anything to do with my not being able to move at a faster pace. The argument put forth about some future, phantom, regulatory impact serving to discourage the starting of Small Businesses is also pure B.S!!! A guy who can be so easily discouraged was never a "Businessman" in the first place. So, we are back to the jobs report and what it means to the election. Given the fact that 8.5 million jobs were lost under the 8 years of the Bush administration... I honestly don't understand how an argument can be made that since there were "ONLY" 94,000 jobs created last month, that is somehow a signal that we should abandon the path of job creation we are now on, and have been moving on under President Obama, and run back to the path of total job destruction, to the tune of 800,000 jobs a month, 800,000 jobs/month!!! which we are moving away from, can possibly make any sense to anyone who is not completely blinded by bias in favor of a republican agenda, no matter how foolish, impertinent, and destructive. The banks are not lending to business. Therefore business cannot expand. Giving billionaires another tax-cut will not reverse this trend, but will encourage those billionaires to continue investing off-shore, i.e., Singapore, China, Brazil, anywhere but the USA. How long before we admit this and move forward??? This is why the jobs trend is so sluggish."

9/11/12

What will be the triggers for the rest of the year for a possible financial crisis and the consequences in global and US finance?

Well there are several. Let's list a few first and the go back after for the detail.

1. 70% of the trades on Wall Street are by computer. Computer glitches real or manipulated can set off a panic and that can make valuations and pricing difficult if not impossible, including gold, silver and stocks.

2. The Greek default could result in currency to debasement. This would have a domino effect in the west. If not Greece then if Spain asks for a postponement of its austerity programs. Both could trigger in a month or two.

3. The rising price of fuel and food is what actually set off the "Arab Spring" riots. Egypt is at that point again. The most dangerous point for a country as far as bloody revolution is concerned is when seeming gains are followed by severe setbacks.

It was fuel prices and food price increases which set off the Arab spring and it will be rising food and fuel prices that will do it again. How close are they to more increases?

Close.

Governments around the world subsidize fuel and food prices already to avoid revolution. These two plus arms purchases are what they spend their money on.

4. April is the deadline when the US government receipts in taxation come in. If lower than anticipated then expect the US credit rating to drop and interest rates to drop below zero etc., and perhaps a run on US securities and perhaps bonds as well.

5. December 31st. This is the "cliff" deadline which I have written about in other places on this site. Up for action are the tax breaks for the rich, taxes on the middle class, tax cuts for the military and other bread and butt er items.

No telling what will happen. Uncertainty can really trigger ancillary events, most unpleasant.

Five more triggers set to fizzle or ignite in the next six days on Wall Street, the banks and JP Morgan--one pundits view.

http://www.marketwatch.com/story/is-this-a-week-to-remember-or-forget-2012-09-05?link=MW_story_investinginsight

We will throw these into the mix and get back our analysis tomorrow.

But what should the average citizen do about the above situations? Stay tuned.

9/8/12
Should we be buying gold, go on the gold standard as Ron Paul suggests, allow currency collapse and start over again, or impeach congress, end fractional banking and wall street gambling on margin, end buying stock buying on margin on margin-end the Federal Reserve.

Here are some ideas being tossed around and then come back and I will give my suggested solutions/

http://rt.com/programs/keiser-report/episode-338-max-keiser/

12/20/13

Deficit-Cutting: What The American Press Doesn't Tell You.

"Current account deficit smallest in four years

WASHINGTON Tue Dec 17, 2013 8:31am EST

People shop at holiday vendors near Central Park in New York December 14, 2013.

Credit: Reuters/Eric Thayer

 WASHINGTON (Reuters) - The U.S. current account deficit was the smallest in four years in the third quarter as exports increased and more income was earned abroad, a government report showed on Tuesday."

See link below:

http://www.reuters.com/article/2013/12/17/us-current-account-deficit-idUSBRE9BG0OE20131217

 But what does it mean?

Other links on whether our deficit is shrinking or growing?

http://www.people-press.org/2013/12/19/in-deficit-debate-public-resists-cuts-in-entitlements-and-aid-to-poor/

http://www.tcdailyplanet.net/blog/hindsight/federal-spending-whence-comes-deficit

RT TV show

http://rt.com/on-air/

The Family Bank

We, in this country, are looking for answers. I have blogged on this site offering what I think will put this country back on track.
One blog is "What America Needs to Do To Survive?"
Another is on Obama, offering him advice on what needs to be done.
This one is yet another aspect of what can be done to turn things around.
It is the family bank.
The short summary is: Don't give your money to wall street every day, start your own family bank.

The Family Bank idea is to teach families how to

organize themselves into being a bank for the immediate and extended family. Formed as a non-profit, the Family Bank would:

1-Assess family members small payments of five dollars a month in exchange for the right to borrow up to 300 dollars in a revolving loan fund.

2-Participate in a savings fund for the children and the elderly and for family emergencies.

3-Participate in an investment program for the family

4-Being an non-profit, the Bank could solicit grants and tax-free donations and ultimately start to help other families as well.

I did this in Berkeley years ago and that worked very well, eventually families accumulated money to provide security for family members in as little as three years while taking care of immediate needs.

No family member should be living isolated, poor, with no security. A Family Bank can help, especially if many such banks are organized. Family Banks often traded services eliminating the need for money between them. That helped.

Anyway, it's time to put our money into family banks, instead of wall street banks.

Any given family member, with some resources, can start a bank with as little as 200 dollars.
All profits go to fund family projects. In Berkeley, each

family of any size sub-divided the work into sub-committees to reduce time allotments.

Now with the internet, banking transactions among family members could be handled on a Family Bank website, or an existing one utilizing Pay Pal.

Much easier to do these days.

 For a video on the idea click on the link below:

http://www.youtube.com/watch?v=5t5mlP0bjVQ

10-1-11
Here is more detail on how the FB would work:

It can be an entirely on line operation. There are many on-line banks in operation already. Don't need an office or advertising, just a way to deposit and transfer loan monies or an account for savings.

First an individual, like me for example, a Dad transfers money, in this case say 5k dollars on an account which lives on my web site.

Individual B, say my daughter or son needs to quickly borrow 300 dollars. They can borrow the money however, only after joining the family bank paying say 10 or 15 dollars a month, that is depositing it (say via PayPal) or from their own bank in the Family Bank accounts having their name.

Once a member they become eligible for loans say after three payments or a total of 30 dollars.

They go to the web site, request the loan, and then the money, after approval, is transferred to their account at the Family Bank ready for transfer to their own bank or they could use the money to pay bills right there on the FB web site.

The money could be paid back on a flexible schedule but it must be paid back in order for the individual to be eligible for a new loan.

So with 30 family members the FB has 300 plus 5000 dollars on day one when it opens up on line.

The interest rate on loans is no interest, or a maximum of three percent.

The profits go back into the FB.

Now the money the FB has can really grow quickly under the following scenarios:

Donations and grant money can be solicited, in connection with helping other families set up a similar FB

I, or a family member, rather than deposit my paychecks into Wells Fargo or greedy bank number two, would deposit my paycheck into the FB bank. If several family members do this the FB could open with 10 or 15k in the accounts useable for loans and emergencies.

Say that adds 5,000 extra dollars a month to the FB, money now available for loans.
The FB in the first one to three months would have over ten thousand available for loans, or the money could be

put into a family investment account, or to help the poor in the family or whatever.

How do I pay my bills if the money is not in Wells Fargo Bank? The same way you do it now by transferring the funds online to your vendor on line.

If you don't want that hassle, this need could be a job for a family member, a stay at home job for a small fee could see that bills got paid. People don't know it but Visa and Master card will issue cards to individuals and organizations, not just to banks.

Trust is a factor here, of course, and some family members might not be entrusted with the family finances.

What if a borrower doesn't pay back. Well then no more loans until the money is paid back.

Emergency loans, funerals and such could be handled differently.

Also time banking could be a way of paying off a loan. Person A goes and takes care of Grandma for a few weeks as a way of paying off a loan.

Services could be used where person A has no cash and services could be directly exchanged among family members. Job leads, borrowing cars, adding a family member to insurance policies are ways of relating that save family members money and constitute a gigantic self-help organization.

Family members would have to agree to serve on various family committees helping to make decisions on the various financial projects identified above.

Who needs money for college, how can the FB help?

The advantage of the FB is that the family instead of putting thousands of dollars each month into wall street banks who use our own money against us , we put the money into our own family banks and use that money for our own benefit and cut out the profit wall street banks take from us. This is thousands of dollars each year in interest we pay the greedy who give us nothing in return.

We regain control of our own lives and our own money. And did I mention that if a claustrophobe hits like flood, earthquake and such, groups of family banks can make the difference help each other with loans and support, housing and such without waiting for FEMA to show up.

And if enough families did this, say 100,000 we could also bring Wall Street down or effect real change in this country. There is nothing that terrifies a banker more than a threat to take our money from them.

Besides, in the case of something like the down payment on a house the kids save thousands of dollar paid out to banks in interest, have a much lower mortgage which they pay to the FB not Wall Street.

There is a family board of directors, the kids can take over the bank and some can get a real paying job handling the bank, as the non-profit, or in the foundation side of things and the families future is much more secure.

That is a quick summary of how it can work.

October 20th I will make the first deposit in the FB to get things rolling.

 For a real education of how commercial and wall street banks really work to profit from your money click on the link below. Also see my blog on this site "Wall Street, the Banks, The Government"

http://www.youtube.com/watch?v=ArfPytAoeZ0&feature=related

Those interested in learning more can message me on this site or at my website: www.lonniehicks.com

www.ingramcontent.com/pod-product-compliance
Lightning Source LLC
Chambersburg PA
CBHW060159290526
45789CB00003B/1087